EXPLORING DINOSAURS

MAIASAURA

By Susan H. Gray

THE CHILD'S WORLD®
CHANHASSEN, MINNESOTA

The Child's World

Published in the United States of America by The Child's World®
PO Box 326, Chanhassen, MN 55317-0326
800-599-READ
www.childsworld.com

Photo Credits: Interior photographs and artwork: Corbis: 5, 9, 10 (William Manning), 11 (Dewitt Jones), 13 (Layne Kennedy), 27 (Danny Lehman); Douglas Henderson: 6, 14, 16, 18, 19, 20, 24-top and bottom; Getty Images/Time Life Pictures: 12; Michael Skrepnick: 15, 17, 25; NASA/Johnson Spaceflight Center/AdTech Photo Imaging: 22; Photo Researchers/Chase Scenic: 8.

Content Adviser:
Peter Makovicky,
Ph.D., Curator,
Field Museum,
Chicago, Illinois

The Child's World®: Mary Berendes, Publishing Director

Editorial Directions, Inc.: E. Russell Primm, Editorial Director; Ruth M. Martin, Line Editor; Katie Marsico, Assistant Editor; Matthew Messbarger, Editorial Assistant; Susan Hindman, Copy Editor; Susan Ashley, Proofreader; Tim Griffin, Indexer; Kerry Reid, Fact Checker; Cian Loughlin O'Day, Photo Reseacher; Linda S. Koutris, Photo Selector

Original cover art by Todd Marshall

The Design Lab: Kathleen Petelinsek, Design and Art Direction; Kari Thornborough, Page Production

Library of Congress Cataloging-in-Publication Data
Gray, Susan Heinrichs.
  Maiasaura / by Susan H. Gray.
      p. cm. — (Exploring dinosaurs)
Includes index.
Summary: Describes what is known about the physical characteristics, behavior, habitat, and life cycle of this plant-eating, duck-billed dinosaur.
  ISBN 1-59296-188-6 (lib. bdg. : alk. paper)
  1. Maiasaura—Juvenile literature. [1. Maiasaura. 2. Dinosaurs.] I. Title. II. Series.
QE862.O65G7456 2004
567.914—dc22   2003018627

Table of Contents

CHAPTER ONE

WAITING

It was a warm spring afternoon. The morning rains had washed everything clean. Sparkling beads of water clung to the ferns. Dinosaur footprints covered the soft ground. Each print was filled with muddy water.

Maiasaura (MY-uh-SAWR-uh) looked up and gazed across the land. Dozens of other *Maiasaura* busily tended their nests. Some gently shaped their nesting mounds out of mud. Others covered their eggs with plants or leaves.

In the distance, a group of young dinosaurs munched on ground plants. Suddenly, they stopped and stood straight up. Each one was tense and alert. But it was a false alarm. After a few seconds, they went back to their meal.

Not far away, another group of youngsters had just hatched.

They were seeing the world for the first time. They blinked,

stretched, and tumbled from the nest. Their mother tried her

best to keep her babies together.

It's lunchtime for Maiasaura! *Ferns would have been a plentiful food source for* Maiasaura *during the late Cretaceous period.*

Maiasaura *doesn't mean "good mother lizard" for nothing. Much evidence exists to suggest that female* Maiasaura *were tender and nurturing parents.*

Maiasaura

looked down at

her own nest.

Twenty-four eggs

were safely buried

in the mound. She

watched for signs

of movement. She

turned her head and

listened for the soft-

est sounds. Not yet,

but soon. Then she

lay down next to the

mound and waited.

CHAPTER TWO

WHAT IS A MAIASAURA?

Maiasaura is a dinosaur that lived from about 80 million to 75 million years ago. Its name is taken from Greek words that mean "good mother lizard." It was given this name because adult and baby skeletons were found together. The finding led scientists to believe that this dinosaur was a "good mother" who cared for her young.

Maiasaura grew to a length of about 30 feet (9 meters). As an adult, it may have weighed as much as 3 or 4 tons. Its back legs were much longer than its front ones. The **reptile** probably walked about on four legs as it fed on plants. When it had to escape **predators,** it probably reared up and ran on its back legs. The dinosaur had a thick, heavy tail and a broad

The Cretaceous period saw a great diversity among the dinosaurs. Huge, horn-faced plant eaters lived alongside small, agile meat-eating dinosaurs.

neck. As it ran, it held its tail and head almost straight out to stay balanced.

Maiasaura's head was long and flattened. Its mouth looked a little like a duck's beak. For this reason, *Maiasaura* and its cousins are called duck-billed dinosaurs.

Maiasaura had no teeth in the front of its mouth. But the back of its mouth was loaded with them. Rows and rows of teeth filled its jaws. New teeth were constantly pushing in to replace old, worn-out ones. An adult's mouth could be packed with well over a thousand teeth.

The dinosaur probably had excellent eyesight. It had sharp hearing and a good sense of smell. These senses kept *Maiasaura* alert to everything in its **environment.**

A hadrosaurid *jawbone.* Hadrosaurs *(or "bulky lizards") were duck-billed* herbivores. Maiasaura *is a member of the* Hadrosaurid *family.*

CHAPTER THREE

WHO FOUND THE FIRST *MAIASAURA?*

A family of **fossil** hunters first discovered *Maiasaura* skeletons.

The mother of the family was Marion Brandvold. Even as a

child in Montana, Marion kept her eyes on the ground. She loved to

hunt for fossils, unusual rocks, and arrowheads. To Marion, nothing

was better than spending a day in the fields and hills. As an adult, she

continued to collect things she found on the ground. Some rocks that

Maiasaura lived in the area that we now know as Montana. The Maiasaura *bones found there represented one of the most important fossil discoveries of the 20th century.*

she found she kept for herself. She put others up for sale in her rock shop in Bynum, Montana.

Trilobites are an extinct group of sea animals that were alive during the Paleozoic era. Many Trilobite fossils such as the one shown here were found in Montana.

Marion's son David Trexler grew to share her interest. As soon as he learned to walk, David went fossil hunting with his mom. Even when he grew up and married, he kept looking for fossils. His wife, Laurie, often joined in the family fossil hunts.

It was during one of these hunts in the 1970s that Marion found some baby dinosaur skeletons. Many of the bones were broken. She took some of them home and spread them out. She and David began fitting the little bones together.

One day, a scientist came into Marion's shop. His name was Jack Horner. He looked at all of her rocks and fossils. Then Marion showed

Jack Horner not only named Maiasaura *and discovered the first* Maiasaura *eggs ever found, but he is also the curator of paleontology at the Museum of the Rockies in Bozeman, Montana. He has authored six books on dinosaurs and even served as technical adviser for the movies* Jurassic Park *and* The Lost World.

him the little dinosaur bones.

Horner was amazed. He knew right away that they came from baby dinosaurs. He also knew that they were from a new kind of dinosaur no one had ever found before.

Horner brought other people to Montana to look for more bones from the mysterious dinosaur. During one hunt, Laurie Trexler found an adult skeleton. It was clearly the same kind of dinosaur as the babies. Horner gave it the name *Maiasaura*. The dinosaur became known as a good mother. Marion Brandvold was a good mother as well. She gave her son and many other people a love of rocks and fossils.

WHAT WERE DINOSAUR MOMS LIKE?

For years, paleontologists (PAY-lee-un-TAWL-uh-jists) disagreed over dinosaur mothers. Paleontologists are people who study **ancient** life. They study bones and footprints that animals have left behind. They look at leaf imprints in rocks. They study the environments of long-dead animals. They compare these animals to animals living today. Then they try to figure out how ancient animals lived and how they're related to today's animals.

Paleontologists had different ideas about dinosaur mothers. Many believed dinosaurs acted like some reptiles of today. They thought that mothers laid eggs, then

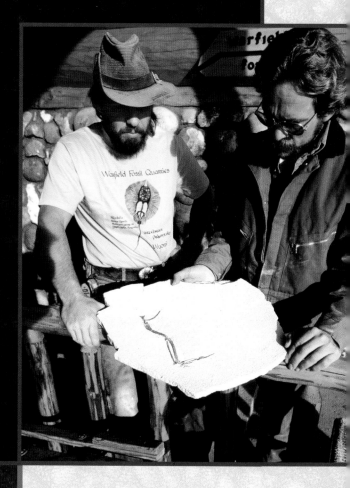

just walked away. When babies hatched, they had to make it on their own.

Other paleontologists felt differently. They believed that mothers took care of their young. Then after a while, the babies could take care of themselves. There was just one prob- lem with this idea. There was no proof.

The discovery of *Maiasaura* changed every- thing. At last, scientists saw fossils of adult and baby dinosaurs that lived together. This does not prove that *all* dinosaurs were good parents. But at least some of them were.

CHAPTER FOUR

WHAT DO *MAIASAURA* NESTS TELL US?

Many *Maiasaura* nests have been discovered. The dinosaur's nests were actually mounds of mud. Each mound was about 7 feet (2 m) wide. The top of each mound sank in, forming a shallow bowl. The eggs were laid in the bowl so they did not roll away. A nest usually held up to 25 eggs. Each egg was about the size of a grapefruit.

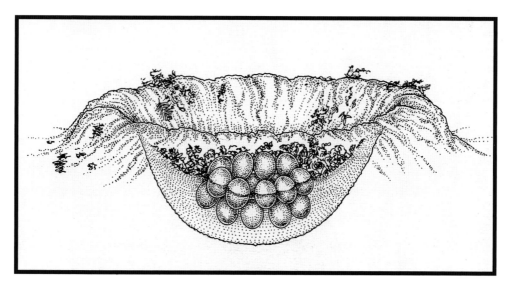

Maiasaura *nests were holes scooped out of the ground.* Maiasaura *babies could not take care of themselves when they were newlyhatched. They probably stayed in the nest for a long time.*

The remains of Maiasaura *babies revealed worn teeth. This suggests that they were fed by their parents until they were old enough to leave the nest.*

Maiasaura built many nests over a large area of ground. This means that they must have lived close together in a big group. The nests were not crowded together, however. The dinosaurs built nests about 30 feet (9 m) apart. Thirty feet is about the length of one adult *Maiasaura.* So they left just enough room between nests to get around.

Mothers probably did not sit on the eggs to keep them warm. After all, a *Maiasaura* weighed several tons! Instead, they might have placed plants or leaves over the eggs. As plants rot, they give off heat.

The heat may have been just enough to keep the eggs warm. Certain crocodiles and birds of today use rotting plants in the same way.

Some *Maiasaura* nests that have been found are loaded with chips of eggshells. This is probably because the baby dinosaurs stayed in the nests for a long time, stepping all over their own shells. **Nestlings** were too little to go out and get their own food. So their parents had to stay around and feed them. In time, the youngsters grew big enough to feed themselves.

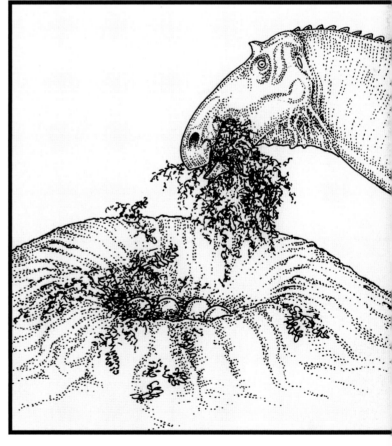

Maisaura *gently placed moss, earth, and leaves on top of her eggs. As the material rotted, it gave off heat and kept the eggs warm.*

CHAPTER FIVE

WHAT WERE THE BABIES LIKE?

Maiasaura **hatchlings** were pretty helpless. They were about 1 foot (30 centimeters) long and could not walk very well. They weighed around 1.5 pounds (0.7 kilograms), about as much as a head of lettuce. Parents brought food such as leaves and berries to the little babies.

Many kinds of dinosaurs had babies that were able to fend for themselves when very young, but Maiasaura *babies were mothered for a long time before becoming self-sufficient.*

There is strong evidence to suggest that Maiasaura *traveled in groups. One reason for this might be that they could better protect themselves by staying close to one another in case of attack.*

Even as the young dinosaurs grew, they probably did not wander far from home. Paleontologists believe this because young dinosaurs' skeletons were found right alongside those of adults. Bones of babies, youngsters, and adults have all been found together in the same area. When animals of all ages live together, it is called a colony.

It is safer for young animals to live in a colony than all alone. In a colony, a few animals can warn the others of danger. Some-times the bigger animals will surround and protect the smaller

A hungry meat-eating dinosaur would have been no match for several Maiasaura *ready to defend themselves and their colony.*

ones. Young *Maiasaura* might have grown into adults in the

colony they were born into. Others might have started their own

colonies. Whatever they did, little *Maiasaura* had to grow up fast.

In fact, most dinosaurs probably grew up quickly. Otherwise,

they were in danger of becoming some other dinosaur's meal.

Many paleontologists believe that *Maiasaura* were adults by the

time they were five years old. If this is true, a young *Maiasaura*

gained more than 1,000 pounds (454 kg) a year!

A BIG YEAR FOR *MAIASAURA*

The year 1985 was a big one for *Maiasaura*. In that year, the dinosaur was named the state fossil of Montana. It also became the first dinosaur to travel into space.

It was in Montana that Marion Brandvold found the first *Maiasaura* bones. So the people of Montana wanted to honor the dinosaur. They wanted *Maiasaura* to be named the state fossil. Montana schoolchildren got involved in this project. They wrote letters to the governor. They signed petitions. They even made 2,000 dinosaur cookies and served them to state lawmakers. Finally, their work paid off. The governor signed the State Fossil Bill, and *Maiasaura* became famous all over Montana.

A few months later, *Maiasaura* made the news again. Every year, scientists travel into space on the space shuttle. Often they take treasures from home with them. Some take gifts from their children. Some take things to remind them of their town or state. In 1985, astronaut Loren Acton wanted to take something really special on his 8-day mission into

space. He decided to take pieces of *Maiasaura* bones and eggshells. They belonged to Montana State University, where Acton went to school. Everyone agreed this was a great idea. So the fossils were carefully stowed on the spacecraft. When the shuttle took off, *Maiasaura* became the first dinosaur to travel in space.

CHAPTER SIX

How Did *MAIASAURA* Spend Its Time?

An animal with an enormous body to feed probably spends most of its time eating. This was surely the case for *Maiasaura.* The dinosaur was an herbivore (UR-buh-vore). This means that it ate plants.

Maiasaura's mouth was built especially for plant-eating. Its hard, toothless beak was perfect for nipping small branches from bushes and trees. The teeth at the back of its jaws ground the materials to bits. Finding and eating plants took up most of the animal's day. Just to stay alive, an adult had to eat hundreds of pounds of plants every week!

Large *Maiasaura* colonies probably moved from place to place to find food. They tore plants up by the roots and yanked branch-

A stampede of Maiasaura *comes crashing through the lush land.*

This is a picture of what Maiasaura *and their young might have looked like as they fed on plants and berries.*

es from trees. They ate everything they could and then moved on. They may have returned to the same spot every year, though, to build nests and lay eggs. These *Maiasaura* colonies were enormous. In Montana, paleontologists found a group of about 10,000 skeletons in one area.

The huge reptiles had their enemies, too. Their predators probably included *Saurornitholestes* (SORE-or-

NITH-oh-LESS-tees) and *Albertosaurus* (al-BURT-uh-SAWR-us).

These fierce meat eaters had sharp teeth and claws that could easily

tear *Maiasaura*'s flesh. However, a colony of 10,000 *Maiasaura*

might have been enough to make such attackers think twice.

Scientists think that carnivores like Albertosaurus *may have hunted in packs. This would have given them an advantage when attacking plant eaters such as* Maiasaura *and the* Hypacrosaurus *(hi-PACK-roh-SAWR-us) pictured here.*

CHAPTER SEVEN

WHATEVER BECAME OF *MAIASAURA*?

Maiasaura was among the last dinosaurs on Earth. It lived in the western part of North America during the Cretaceous (kreh-TAY-shuss) period. This period lasted from about 144 million to 65 million years ago.

At the time, the Earth was very different from today. At the beginning of the Cretaceous period, the Earth was fairly warm. Toward the end of the period, the Earth began to cool. As time went on, many different kinds of plants developed. Trees and flowering plants appeared and spread.

Maiasaura died out as the Cretaceous period was coming to an end. In fact, by the end of the period, all the dinosaurs had died out. Not a single one was left on Earth. No one is quite sure why this happened.

Fortunately, dinosaur fossils have remained to this day. Bones, footprints, and nests are still here for us to study. They may not tell us why *Maiasaura* died. But they can tell us much about how the dinosaur lived.

Footprints such as this one are part of the geological evidence that tells us about the time that Maiasaura *roamed Earth.*

Glossary

ancient (AYN-shunt) Something that is ancient is very old; from millions of years ago. Paleontology is the study of ancient plant and animal life.

environment (en-VYE-ruhn-muhnt) An environment is made up of the things that surround a living creature, such as the air and soil. *Maiasaura* had to keep aware of its environment to find food and to avoid its enemies.

fossil (FOSS-uhl) A fossil is the remains of an ancient plant or animal. People hunt for fossils because they tell us a lot about life on Earth long ago.

hatchlings (HACH-lingz) Hatchlings are baby animals that have just hatched from eggs. Many hatchlings cannot take care of themselves right away.

nestlings (NEST-lingz) Nestlings are baby animals still living in a nest. A *Maiasaura* nestling was fed by its parents.

predators (PRED-uh-turz) Predators are animals that hunt and eat other animals. *Maiasaura* escaped its predators by running away.

reptile (REP-tile) A reptile is an air-breathing animal with a backbone and is usually covered with scales or plates. *Maiasaura* was a reptile.

Did You Know?

▶ Discoveries of baby dinosaur skeletons are quite rare.

▶ So many dinosaur eggs have been found at one place in Montana that it is called Egg Mountain. This is where *Maiasaura* skeletons and nests were first discovered.

▶ A museum in Bozeman, Montana, now has the *Maiasaura* fossils that went into space.

TRIASSIC PERIOD

Date: 248 million to 208 million years ago

Fossils: *Coelophysis, Cynodont, Desmatosuchus, Eoraptor, Gerrothorax, Peteinosaurus, Placerias, Plateosaurus, Postosuchus, Procompsognathus, Riojasaurus, Saltopus, Teratosaurus, Thecodontosaurus*

Distinguishing Features: For the most part, the climate in the Triassic period was hot and dry. The first true mammals appeared during this period, as well as turtles, frogs, salamanders, and lizards. Corals could also be found in oceans at this time, although large reefs such as the ones we have today did not yet exist. Evergreen trees made up much of the plant life.

JURASSIC PERIOD

Date: 208 million to 144 million years ago

Fossils: *Allosaurus, Anchisaurus, Apatosaurus, Barosaurus, Brachiosaurus, Ceratosaurus, Compsognathus, Cryptoclidus, Dilophosaurus, Diplodocus, Eustreptospondylus, Hybodus, Janenschia, Kentrosaurus, Liopleurodon, Megalosaurus, Opthalmosaurus, Rhamphorhynchus, Saurolophus, Segisaurus, Seismosaurus, Stegosaurus, Supersaurus, Syntarsus, Ultrasaurus, Vulcanodon, Xiaosaurus*

Distinguishing Features: The climate of the Jurassic period was warm and moist. The first birds appeared during this period. Plant life was also greener and more widespread. Sharks began swimming in Earth's oceans. Although dinosaurs didn't even exist at the beginning of the Triassic period, they ruled Earth by Jurassic times. There was a minor mass extinction toward the end of the Jurassic period.

CRETACEOUS PERIOD

Date: 144 million to 65 million years ago

Fossils: *Acrocanthosaurus, Alamosaurus, Albertosaurus, Anatotitan, Ankylosaurus, Argentinosaurus, Bagaceratops, Baryonyx, Carcharodontosaurus, Carnotaurus, Centrosaurus, Chasmosaurus, Corythosaurus, Didelphodon, Edmontonia, Edmontosaurus, Gallimimus, Gigantosaurus, Hadrosaurus, Hypsilophodon, Iguanodon, Kronosaurus, Lambeosaurus, Leaellynasaura, Maiasaura, Megaraptor, Muttaburrasaurus, Nodosaurus, Ornithocheirus, Oviraptor, Pachycephalosaurus, Panoplosaurus, Parasaurolophus, Pentaceratops, Polacanthus, Protoceratops, Psittacosaurus, Quaesitosaurus, Saltasaurus, Sarcosuchus, Saurolophus, Sauropelta, Saurornithoides, Saurornitholestes, Segnosaurus, Spinosaurus, Stegoceras, Stygimoloch, Styracosaurus, Tapejara, Tarbosaurus, Therizinosaurus, Thescelosaurus, Torosaurus, Trachodon, Triceratops, Troodon, Tyrannosaurus rex, Utahraptor, Velociraptor*

Distinguishing Features: The climate of the Cretaceous period was fairly mild. Flowering plants first appeared in this period, and many modern plants developed. With flowering plants came a greater diversity of insect life. Birds further developed into two types: flying and flightless. A wider variety of mammals also existed. At the end of this period came a great mass extinction that wiped out the dinosaurs, along with several other groups of animals.

How to Learn More

At the Library

Maynard, Christopher. *The Best Book of Dinosaurs.*
New York: Larousse Kingfisher Chambers, 1998.

Sandell, Elizabeth J. *Maiasaura: The Good Mother Dinosaur.*
Naples, Fla.: Bancroft Sage, 1989.

On the Web

Visit our home page for lots of links about *Maiasaura:*
http://www.childsworld.com/links.html
Note to Parents, Teachers, and Librarians: We routinely verify our
Web links to make sure they're safe, active sites—so encourage
your readers to check them out!

Places to Visit or Contact

AMERICAN MUSEUM OF NATURAL HISTORY
*To view numerous dinosaur fossils, as well
as the fossils of several ancient mammals*
Central Park West at 79th Street
New York, NY 10024-5192
212/769-5100

CARNEGIE MUSEUM OF NATURAL HISTORY
*To view a variety of dinosaur skeletons, as well as fossils related
to other reptiles, amphibians, and fish that are now extinct*
4400 Forbes Avenue
Pittsburgh, PA 15213
412/622-3131

DINOSAUR NATIONAL MONUMENT
To view a huge deposit of dinosaur bones in a natural setting
Dinosaur, CO 81610-9724
or
Dinosaur National Monument (Quarry)
11625 East 1500 South
Jensen, UT 84035
435/781-7700

MUSEUM OF THE ROCKIES
To see several exhibits related to Maiasaura
Montana State University
600 West Kagy Boulevard
Bozeman, MT 59717-2730
406/994-2251 or 406/994-DINO (3466)

NATIONAL MUSEUM OF NATURAL HISTORY
(SMITHSONIAN INSTITUTION)
To see several dinosaur exhibits and special behind-the-scenes tours
10th Street and Constitution Avenue, N.W.
Washington, D.C. 20560-0166
202/357-2700

Index

About the Author

Susan H. Gray has bachelor's and master's degrees in zoology, and has taught college-level courses in biology. She first fell in love with fossil hunting while studying paleontology in college. In her 25 years as an author, she has written many articles for scientists and researchers, and many science books for children. Susan enjoys gardening, traveling, and playing the piano. She and her husband, Michael, live in Cabot, Arkansas.